GRILLING

50 Recipes from the
Chicago Tribune

TRIBUNE
PUBLISHING

ORLANDO / 1993

CHICAGO TRIBUNE

Carol Haddix: Food Guide Editor
and the food staff of the *Chicago Tribune*

Cover photograph by Bill Hogan
Back cover photograph by Tony Berardi

Inside photographs by
Tony Berardi, Bob Fila,
Bill Hogan, John Dziekan

Cover design by Bill Henderson,
Tribune Publishing

Copyright © 1993
Tribune Publishing
75 East Amelia Street
Orlando, Florida 32801

Printed in the United States

FIRST EDITION

Library of Congress
Cataloging-in-Publication Data
Grilling : 50 recipes from the Chicago tribune.
     p.   cm.
   Includes index.
   ISBN 1-56943-003-9
   1. Barbecue cookery.   I. Chicago tribune.
TX840.B3G749   1993
641.5'784--dc20   93-4527
                 CIP

TRIBUNE PUBLISHING

Editorial Director: George C. Biggers III
Managing Editor: Dixie Kasper
Senior Editor: Kathleen M. Kiely
Production Editor: Ken Paskman
Designer: Bill Henderson

For information:
Tribune Publishing
P.O. Box 1100
Orlando, Florida 32801

Thanks go to the following people for their help
in producing this book, as well as the
Tribune's weekly newspaper food section and columns:

Jack Fuller, Joe Leonard, Howard Tyner,
Brenda Butler, Connie Coning, Steven Pratt,
JeanMarie Brownson, Pat Dailey, William Rice,
Barbara Sullivan, Patti Florez, Dianne Hugh,
Kevin Fewell, Bob Fila, Bill Hogan, Tony Berardi,
John Dziekan, Karen Blair,
Mary Wilson and Terry Smith.

– *Carol Haddix*

Fickle food trends come and go, but grilling over burning embers is here to stay. After all, the concept goes back to when people first experimented with food and fire, and decided cooked food tasted better than raw.

Since then, outdoor cooking over a grill has evolved into a cuisine of its own. Whether we are grilling foods with an Italian, Caribbean or Mexican bent, it is that unique flavor of cooking directly over fire that Americans love.

Today, more than 77 percent of American households own grills, and 90 percent of those have used them at least once in the past year, according to the Barbecue Industry Association.

What are we grilling? Mostly hamburgers, chicken, steaks and hot dogs or sausages. But many unusual items also flock to the flame, including ethnic appetizers such as Thai chicken on skewers, pizza, entrees such as Korean beef or Mexican red snapper, and even side dishes of grilled fresh fruit or vegetables.

Within the pages of this cookbook you'll find 50 recipes for some of these exotic dishes, as well as for simple grilled meats, poultry and fish. All of the recipes have appeared in the *Chicago Tribune*. While most of them will turn out best when cooked outdoors over charcoal or wood, they also can be adapted to indoor cooking under a broiler with just a small adjustment in the timing. To help make your menu planning easier, we have included a few side dishes that are not cooked on the grill but that go well with barbecued foods.

HOT TIPS FOR GRILLING

Patience is the most important technique required for grilling most foods: patience to allow the coals to preheat properly, and patience to let the food cook at a moderate temperature to prevent scorching and overcooking. Whether you are entertaining guests or grilling for the family, these basics will help ensure a successful cookout:

SELECTING A GRILL

Outdoor grills come in three basic styles. Although gas and electric grills are preferred by many for their ease of use, charcoal grills continue to be the most popular.

Uncovered grills and hibachis are better for any food that cooks less than 25 minutes. They have the added advantage of allowing the cook to change the distance between the cooking grate and the heat source.

Covered grills generally do not have adjustable cooking grates. However, the heat level can be changed by varying the number of coals used and adjusting the air vents. More air keeps the fire hotter, less air means a cooler grill. An oven thermometer can be used to help maintain an even temperature.

A covered grill is ideal for food requiring a long cooking time, such as large pieces of meat or whole poultry. It also helps impart a smoky flavor to food. A tip: Keep a small area of the grill free of coals so any food cooking too quickly can be moved there.

SETTING UP THE GRILL

For gas and electric grills, follow the manufacturer's directions.

To fuel a charcoal grill, select from briquets, hardwood lump charcoal or hardwood. Save other items, such as wood chips, grapevine cuttings and fruitwood cuttings used for flavoring, until after the fuel has heated.

Whichever fuel you use, start the fire at least 25 minutes before putting food on the grill. Ignite the coals with an electric starter, a chimney starter or charcoal lighter fluid, according to package directions. Let the coals burn until evenly covered with a white ash, then cook over the coals, never over the flames.

ARRANGING THE COALS

Direct-heat method: This means the food is cooked directly over the heat source. It is perfect for foods that cook in less than 25 minutes, such as small pieces of meat, steaks, burgers, fish fillets, seafood kebabs, cut-up poultry and vegetables.

Indirect-heat method: This method relies on reflected heat, similar to oven roasting. Almost any food suitable for oven roasting, such as large roasts, whole poultry, whole fish and thick pork chops can be cooked in this manner. After the coals have burned to the white-ash stage, they should be banked equally on opposite sides of the grill with a drip pan between them. The food is positioned on the cooking grate over the drip pan and cooked with the grill covered.

For long-cooking foods such as roasts, turkey and leg of lamb, use an oven thermometer to determine the grill temperature and keep the heat constant.

FLAVORINGS

To add smoke flavor to foods, soak wood chips, such as mesquite, hickory, applewood, olivewood or grapevines, in water to cover for at least 15 minutes. Soak chunks of wood at least 30 minutes. Drain the wood and add it to the hot coals according to taste: Add early in the cooking time for more smoke flavor; add later for a subtle smoke flavor. Cover the grill to create maximum smoke.

Other flavorings include fresh herbs, pecan shells, citrus rinds and lemon grass stalks. These should be added to the coals near the end of cooking. To minimize burning, the flavorings should be soaked in water first.

COOKING

For easier cleanup, remove the cooking grate from the grill before heating and spray with nonstick vegetable spray. Heating the cooking grate before adding the food will help prevent it from sticking.

Turn food with tongs or a flat spatula while cooking; a fork punctures the food, releasing its juices.

Food at room temperature will cook faster than cold food. Most food will come to room temperature in the time it takes for the coals to reach the desired temperature.

Trim excess fat from meat and poultry to help prevent flareups. If flareups do occur, cover the grill to extinguish the flames.

Place a fine grate or wire-mesh screen, sprayed with nonstick vegetable spray, on top of the cooking grate for cooking small, delicate foods such as cut-up vegetables, skewered fruit, small shrimp, scallops and thin fish fillets. Small pieces can also be speared on metal or wooden skewers. Soak wooden skewers in water for at least 20 minutes before cooking to prevent them from burning. A grill basket is handy for cooking whole fish.

The microwave oven can be an invaluable aid to quick and easy barbecuing, especially with chicken and pork. Use the microwave to do most of the cooking ahead of time, then finish the meat on the grill to add flavor and crispness. This method also keeps the meat from drying out after long cooking over the fire.

MEAT

Select meats and chops for grilling that are about $1/2$ inch to 3 inches thick. Thinner meats overcook quickly and tend to dry out. Larger roasts, or boned and tied roasts, should be cooked by the indirect method, but can be seared first over the coals. Trim off most of the fat. Tougher cuts, such as flank steak, beef chuck and lamb shoulder, benefit from marinating in an acidic solution, such as a vinaigrette, for several hours before cooking.

The best way to check for doneness is with an instant-read thermometer. The temperature of large cuts of meat will rise about 10 degrees after they are removed from the grill, so remove them before they reach the desired doneness temperature. Let all meat stand 5 to 10 minutes before cutting to prevent excess juice from escaping.

Beef, lamb and veal will be cooked rare at 130 to 135 degrees; 140 degrees for medium-rare; 150 to 155 degrees for medium; and 160 to 165 degrees for well-done.

Pork will be done at 150 to 155 for medium and 160 to 165 for well-done.

POULTRY

Grill cut-up chicken or Cornish hens over direct heat. First sear them quickly over a hot fire, then cover the grill for the remainder of the cooking. If using a marinade, baste them often.

Apply barbecue sauce near the end of cooking to prevent it from scorching. The skin is best left on grilled poultry to help retain moisture; remove it after cooking if desired.

For whole poultry, truss the bird if desired. Grill whole birds, turkey breasts and delicate game birds over indirect heat. Baste often with marinade or chicken broth. For grilled duck or goose, use a drip pan and cover the grill to prevent flareups.

Measure poultry temperature with an instant-read thermometer in the thickest part of the thigh or breast, but not touching the bones. White meat should be about 160 degrees; dark meat about 170 degrees. The juices should run clear. If a whole bird has been stuffed, the stuffing should be at least 160 degrees in the center.

FISH AND SHELLFISH

Thick fish steaks such as salmon, swordfish, tuna, halibut, shark and marlin are the simplest cuts to grill; select steaks that are 1 to 2 inches thick. Fillets and shellfish also can be grilled successfully with the use of a grill screen or a hinged grate. Fish cooks much faster than meat, and continues cooking after it is removed from the grill.

Fish steaks and fillets can be cooked over direct heat. Larger pieces and whole fish should be seared over direct heat, then cooked over indirect heat with the grill covered.

Fish grilling time, like its oven cooking time, usually is about 10 minutes per inch of thickness. An instant-read thermometer should register about 140 degrees. Cooked fish should have opaque flesh; if it flakes easily, it is overdone.

Shrimp, soft-shell crabs and sea scallops should be cooked with direct heat over a medium-hot fire. They need only be cooked until their flesh turns opaque — longer and they'll toughen.

Cooking times: medium shrimp, 5 to 6 minutes; large shrimp, 6 to 8 minutes; sea scallops, 3 to 5 minutes; soft-shell crabs, 5 to 6 minutes.

Cleaned oysters, clams and mussels in the shell can be put directly on the grate over the coals. Cover the grill and cook until the shells barely open, usually 2 to 3 minutes — longer and they will be tough. Discard those that do not open, which indicates they were not fresh when purchased.

VEGETABLES

Grilled vegetables are one of summer's simple pleasures. Most can be grilled with a minimum of preparation. Peppers, tomatoes, potatoes and onions, for example, can be grilled whole. Cut them up and add seasonings and marinades, and they become even more intriguing. Cut-up squash and eggplant can be brushed with homemade or bottled vinaigrette before grilling for added flavor.

Cook cut-up vegetables on a fine grate over direct heat, turning occasionally, until crisp-tender or however desired.

If you need the grill space for the meat or poultry, grill the quick-cooking vegetables first. Keep them warm while the main course cooks, or serve them at room temperature.

Wrap potatoes and slices of sweet onion in heavy-duty foil with a small pat of butter, or a drizzle of olive oil and a sprinkle of herbs and crushed red pepper flakes. Place the packets near, but not touching, the coals. After 45 to 60 minutes, the potatoes will be tender and provide a satisfying meatless entree or side dish.

PORK

These Western-style barbecued ribs use a little amber or dark lager beer in the sauce, but they taste superb when accompanied by a pilsner, whose mild flavor serves as a foil to the spicy sauce. This one is adapted from a recipe by Carl Jerome, an instructor at the Cooking and Hospitality Institute of Chicago.

Preparation time: 20 minutes
Cooking time: 1 hour and
  45 minutes
Yield: 4 servings

RIBS

4 quarts beef stock or broth

1 can (8 ounces) tomato sauce

$^1/_2$ cup honey

2 tablespoons chili powder

2 slabs spareribs, about 5 pounds total, each cut in half

CHILI SAUCE

1 cup each: ketchup, chili sauce, amber or dark lager beer

$^1/_4$ cup Worcestershire sauce

2 tablespoons each: prepared mustard, brown sugar

$1^1/_2$ teaspoons chili powder

1 teaspoon each: dried oregano, hot pepper sauce

1. Put stock, tomato sauce, honey and chili powder in a pot large enough to hold ribs. Heat to a boil, then add the ribs and simmer, uncovered, over very low heat until tender, about $1^1/_2$ hours.

2. Meanwhile, combine chili sauce ingredients in a medium saucepan, whisking thoroughly. Simmer over low heat 15 minutes. Set aside to cool.

3. When ribs are tender, remove them from cooking liquid and brush all over with sauce. Grill over a medium-hot fire, turning several times and brushing with sauce until they are well glazed, 15 to 20 minutes.

Baby back ribs, as the name suggests, are cut from the back rib section of the pig and are not at all tough. Thus, they can be grilled fairly quickly without any precooking. This sauce combines mustard, honey and fruit in a mixture that, well, babies them.

Preparation time: 10 minutes
Marinating time: 30 minutes
 or more
Cooking time: 20 minutes
Yield: 3 to 4 servings

---

¹/₃ cup honey mustard

3 tablespoons each: peach preserves, vegetable oil, fresh lemon juice

¹/₂ teaspoon minced garlic

Salt, pepper to taste

2 racks baby back pork ribs, about 3 pounds total

1. Mix the mustard, preserves, oil, lemon juice, garlic, salt and pepper. Rub all over the ribs and refrigerate at least 30 minutes before grilling.

2. Grill the ribs over a hot fire for 6 to 10 minutes per side. The sauce burns easily, so watch carefully and turn the ribs as necessary.

"Americans grill, roast and toast over an open fire with a skill that is the envy of cooks the world over," wrote Tribune *food and wine columnist William Rice. But his favorite holiday cookout features a literal mixed grill of sausages made in the styles of Germany, Hungary, Poland, Italy, Spain or even England — "the best of the wurst."*

Preparation time: 10 minutes
Marinating time: 4 hours or longer
Cooking time: 10 minutes
Yield: 4 to 6 servings

---

¹/₂ cup beer

¹/₄ cup vegetable oil

1¹/₂ tablespoons light brown sugar

1 bay leaf, crumbled

¹/₂ teaspoon each: crushed red pepper flakes, ground cumin, minced garlic

¹/₄ teaspoon each: dried thyme, paprika, seasoned salt, ground black pepper

4 pounds sausage, a mixture of varieties such as Italian, German, Polish and Spanish

1. Mix all ingredients except sausage. Pour into a shallow glass dish and add sausages, coating them; cover tightly and refrigerate at least 4 hours or longer.

2. Grill sausages over a hot fire until cooked throughout, 8 to 10 minutes, brushing several times with marinade. Serve with or without buns.

Lifestyles have changed dramatically in the last decade as Americans have become more concerned with their diet. Meat processors and farmers have changed too, offering leaner meats. Today's pork, for instance, is close to beef in its fat and cholesterol content. Barbecuing is a quick way to prepare these leaner cuts of pork, as this recipe illustrates.

Preparation time: 30 minutes
Marinating time: 1 hour
Cooking time: 25 minutes
Yield: 6 servings

MARINADE

^{1}/3 cup red wine

^{1}/4 cup each: olive oil, loosely packed fresh basil or 2 teaspoons dried

1 tablespoon chopped fresh oregano or 1/4 teaspoon dried

1 small clove garlic

6 boneless, center-cut pork chops, about 1 inch thick

MUSHROOM SAUCE

1 pound mushrooms, sliced

2 tablespoons olive oil

1 tablespoon minced shallots

^{1}/2 teaspoon minced garlic

1 can (14^1/2 ounces) diced tomatoes

^{1}/4 cup loosely packed fresh basil, chopped, or 2 teaspoons dried

1 tablespoon minced fresh oregano or ^{1}/4 teaspoon dried

1 tablespoon each: minced parsley, drained capers

^{1}/4 teaspoon each: salt, pepper

1. For marinade, put wine, oil, basil, oregano and garlic in blender or food processor. Process until smooth.

2. Put pork chops in shallow glass dish. Pour marinade over chops. Turn once to coat with marinade. Cover and refrigerate 1 hour.

3. Meanwhile, for mushroom sauce, cook mushrooms in oil in large skillet over high heat until they are browned at the edges, 8 to 10 minutes. Add shallots, garlic, tomatoes and their liquid, basil, oregano and parsley. Heat to boil. Reduce heat. Simmer, stirring, until mixture thickens slightly, about 5 minutes. Add capers, salt and pepper. Keep warm. Sauce can be made a day ahead if desired, covered and refrigerated. Reheat gently before serving.

4. Remove chops from marinade and place on grill over medium-hot fire. Grill, turning once, just until chops are no longer pink in center, 8 to 12 minutes. Serve with sauce.

Pork chops really sizzle on the grill, and never more so than when they are accented with Indian flavors. Center or loin-cut chops can be used, but be sure they're cut at least 3/4 inch thick so they don't dry out. Spiced rice pilaf or lentils are ideal accompaniments.

Preparation time: 15 minutes
Marinating time: 12 hours or longer
Cooking time: 8 to 12 minutes
Yield: 4 servings

$1/3$ cup mango chutney, such as Major Grey's

1 small hot chili pepper, seeded

1 tablespoon fresh lemon juice

1 tablespoon rice wine vinegar or white wine vinegar

1 teaspoon each: ground ginger, curry powder

4 pork chops

1. Combine all ingredients except the pork chops in a blender or food processor; mix until smooth. Transfer to a shallow glass baking dish and add pork chops. Turn so they are well-coated with the marinade; cover and refrigerate 12 hours or overnight.

2. Remove the pork chops from the marinade, letting the excess drip off. Grill over a medium-hot fire, turning several times, just until the pork is cooked in the center, 8 to 12 minutes. Serve hot.

When the burgers-and-brats routine gets a little tired, try a mixed grill, says
Chicago Tribune *food writer Pat Dailey. Just buy smaller amounts of a variety
of meats and fish rather than lots of just one, and use a flavorful bourbon
marinade. While you're at it, brush some vegetables with olive oil and put them
on the grill, too.*

Preparation time: 15 minutes
Marinating time: Several hours or
  overnight
Cooking time: Varies
Yield: 8 to 10 servings

$2/3$ cup bourbon

$1/2$ cup each: vegetable oil, honey

6 tablespoons grainy mustard

$1/4$ cup cider vinegar

2 tablespoons soy sauce

$1^1/2$ teaspoons salt

1 teaspoon hot red pepper sauce

6 to 8 pounds meat, including
whole chickens or chicken parts,
sausages, ribs, pork tenderloin,
flank steak, shrimp or scallops

1. Combine all ingredients except
meat, poultry and seafood in
blender or food processor, and mix
well. Separate meat, poultry and
seafood selections into large plastic
food bags. Add small amount of
marinade to each, seal tightly and
refrigerate several hours or
overnight, turning several times.

2. Remove all items from marinade
and pat dry. Grill over medium-hot
fire until each item is cooked as
desired.

This tender and succulent cut of meat positively shines on the grill. Here, tangy, hot, smoky and sweet flavors add grace notes to a simple preparation. The meat can be served hot or cold and it makes an excellent sandwich.

Preparation time: 10 minutes
Marinating time: 2 hours or more
Cooking time: 15 to 20 minutes
Yield: 4 to 6 servings

---

¹/₂ cup buttermilk

2 cloves garlic, crushed

1 tablespoon red pepper sauce

2 pork tenderloins, about 12 ounces each

4 tablespoons each: honey, spicy mustard

2 tablespoons reduced-sodium soy sauce

Freshly ground pepper to taste

1. Combine the buttermilk, garlic and red pepper sauce in a shallow glass dish large enough to hold the pork. Add the two tenderloins and turn so they are well-coated. Cover and refrigerate at least 2 hours or overnight.

2. In a small dish, combine the honey, mustard, soy sauce and pepper.

3. Remove the pork from the marinade and pat dry. Brush all over with the mustard mixture. Grill over a medium fire, turning occasionally, until the meat is no longer pink in the middle, 15 to 20 minutes. The internal temperature should read 160 degrees.

BEEF AND LAMB

Texas barbecue sauces tend to be spicy.
This one, used with beef ribs, is typical of the Lone Star State.
It is from Ardon Judd, a lawyer in Washington, D.C., who hails from Texas.

Preparation time: 30 minutes
Cooking time: 3 hours
Yield: 3 to 4 servings

---

1 cup each: strong black coffee, ketchup

$1/2$ cup Worcestershire sauce

$1/4$ cup ($1/2$ stick) butter

1 tablespoon each: prepared mustard, sugar, salt, freshly ground black pepper

4 pounds beef ribs (see note)

1. Combine ingredients except ribs in a saucepan; heat to a boil and simmer 30 minutes, stirring occasionally. Let cool, cover and refrigerate until needed, as long as 3 days.

2. Cook beef ribs in large pot of simmering water until almost tender, about 2 hours. Transfer to hot grill.

3. Grill over medium-hot coals about 15 minutes. Turn and cook the other side 15 minutes. Brush both sides with sauce and cook, turning occasionally, 5 to 10 minutes more.

4. Simmer $1^1/2$ cups of the sauce until it is thickened and reduced to 1 cup. Serve the ribs with the thick sauce on the side.

Note: You can also use this sauce to baste chicken, pork or lamb. If basting pork, add $1/4$ cup cider vinegar to the sauce.

*An Asian flavor based on pineapple juice, garlic and ginger adds a welcome kick
to beef kebabs. Serve them over parsley or coconut rice.*

Preparation time: 25 minutes
Marinating time: 4 hours
Cooking time: 8 to 10 minutes
Yield: 3 to 4 servings

MARINADE

3 tablespoons pineapple juice

2 tablespoons each: soy sauce, vegetable oil

1 tablespoon each: red wine vinegar, finely chopped green onion, minced ginger root

1 teaspoon brown sugar

1 clove garlic, minced

KEBABS

12 ounces sirloin tip roast or beef flank steak, cut into 1-inch pieces

1 large onion, cut into 16 pieces

2 zucchini, each cut into 8 slices

4 cherry tomatoes

1. Combine marinade ingredients in a large plastic food bag. Add meat, seal tightly and marinate in the refrigerator 4 hours or overnight.

2. Drain and reserve marinade. Thread meat alternately with onion and zucchini on 10-inch metal or wooden skewers. (If using wooden skewers, first soak in water 20 minutes.). Brush generously with marinade.

3. Grill over a medium-hot fire, brushing several times with marinade, for 4 minutes. Add a cherry tomato to each skewer, turn them over and brush with marinade. Grill until cooked as desired; rare will take about 8 minutes. Serve hot.

Barbecue in Korea is a national art, applied to many varieties of meat. These beef rib steaks are great served with bowls of rice, hot bean paste, soy sauce and a bean sprout salad. You can buy hot bean paste in a Korean grocery. While you're there, pick up some fiery kim chee (pickled cabbage), if you dare.

Preparation time: 20 minutes
Marinating time: 30 minutes
Cooking time: 4 minutes
Yield: 6 servings

---

6 small rib eye steaks, about 6 ounces each (see note)

6 small cloves garlic, minced

$1/3$ cup each: water, Oriental sesame oil, soy sauce

2 tablespoons sugar

Freshly ground black pepper

Romaine lettuce leaves, hot bean paste, soy sauce

1. For easiest slicing, freeze meat until partly solid, about 1 to 2 hours. Using a very sharp knife, slice meat into thin strips large enough that they do not fall through the grill grate; a fine grate is helpful.

2. Mix remaining ingredients in a shallow glass dish. Add the beef strips and spoon marinade over them so they are well coated. Marinate, turning occasionally, for about 30 minutes.

3. Drain marinade. Grill meat over a medium-hot fire, turning once, just until it is crisp on the outside but still pink in the center. This will take 2 to 4 minutes, depending on how thick the meat is.

4. Remove meat from grill to a large platter. Serve on the lettuce leaves if desired; drizzle meat with hot bean paste or additional soy sauce if desired.

Note: Chicken also works well in this recipe. Use breasts, wings or legs.

Flank steak is not only lean, says "Cook It Light" columnist Jeanne Jones, but it is economical and flavorful, especially when you marinate it before grilling. Try this easy Japanese-inspired recipe and you'll agree.

Preparation time: 10 minutes
Standing and marinating time:
 24 hours
Cooking time: 6 to 10 minutes
Yield: 8 servings

1^3/4 cups reduced-sodium soy sauce

3 tablespoons sugar

2 cloves garlic, crushed

1 tablespoon grated fresh ginger root

2 pounds flank steak, trimmed

1. Combine all ingredients except the flank steak and, if you like, refrigerate for 1 day to develop flavor before using.

2. Place flank steak in shallow glass dish; add soy mixture. Marinate for 1 to 2 hours before cooking.

3. Cook over a medium-hot fire to desired doneness; 3 to 5 minutes per side for rare, depending on thickness of steak.

Although there is nothing wrong with simple, grilled hamburgers, it's nice to offer the family an occasional variation. This recipe fits the bill, with unusual flavorings of mint, garlic and lemon and a yogurt sauce.

Preparation time: 30 minutes
Cooking time: 10 minutes
Yield: 6 to 8 servings

---

1 cup plain nonfat yogurt

1 tablespoon each: olive oil, minced parsley, minced fresh mint

1^1/$_2$ teaspoons lemon juice or to taste

1 teaspoon minced garlic

Salt, cayenne pepper

1 ripe tomato, seeded, diced

1 red bell pepper, seeded, diced

^{1}/$_2$ cucumber, peeled, seeded, diced

1^1/$_2$ pounds lean ground beef

1 large egg white

1 teaspoon each: ground cumin, sweet paprika, grated lemon rind

1 red onion, sliced

8 Boston lettuce leaves

6 to 8 hamburger buns or pita bread pockets

1. Mix yogurt, olive oil, parsley, mint, lemon juice, garlic and a pinch each salt and cayenne pepper in small bowl. Combine the tomato, bell pepper and cucumber in another bowl. Cover and refrigerate both bowls until ready to serve.

2. Mix beef, egg white, cumin, paprika, lemon rind, 1/2 teaspoon salt and pinch cayenne pepper in medium bowl. Gently mix; shape into 6 to 8 patties. Grill burgers over hot fire, turning once, to desired doneness, about 10 minutes for medium. At same time, cook onion slices until browned on both sides. Heat the buns on the grill. Keep warm.

3. Place some of the chopped tomato mixture on each bottom bun or in pita pockets. Add a leaf of lettuce, a beef patty and more tomato mixture. Serve yogurt sauce on the side.

Blackening became popular a few years ago when New Orleans chef Paul Prudhomme created blackened redfish. This recipe uses the same fiery seasoning to flavor sirloin steak, but does not call for cooking over intense heat. This method retains more of the flavor of the seasoning mix and less of the typical charred taste.

Preparation time: 15 minutes
Marinating time: 1 hour
Cooking time: 10 minutes
Yield: 4 to 6 servings

---

1 tablespoon each: salt, black pepper, cayenne pepper

2 teaspoons white pepper

$1^1/2$ teaspoons each: garlic powder, ground cumin, dried thyme leaves

1 teaspoon onion powder

2 pounds sirloin steak

$^1/2$ cup (1 stick) unsalted butter, melted

1. Combine the herbs and spices in a small bowl, mixing thoroughly.

2. Let the meat come to room temperature. Brush with melted butter. Sprinkle seasoning mix evenly over steak through a small wire-mesh sieve or strainer. Pat seasoning in with your hands. Carefully turn and repeat on other side. Cover and refrigerate at least 1 hour. (Leftover seasoning may be stored in a tightly covered jar for future use.)

3. Let steak come to room temperature. Cook over hot fire, turning once, to desired doneness, about 10 minutes for medium-rare. Slice thinly.

Jamaican cuisine is characterized by several traditional flavors, not the least of which is the Jamaican pimento berry, an oily allspice that dominates the country's jerk seasoning, says Chicago Tribune *food writer Steven Pratt. This rub is full of fire from scotch bonnet (habanero) chilies. Use fewer chilies and seed and devein them if you want a milder flavor. But no matter what, wear gloves when you work with these incendiary chilies.*

Preparation time: 15 minutes
Marinating time: 10 minutes or
   longer
Grilling time: 15 to 20 minutes
Yield: 4 servings

---

1 onion, finely chopped

6 green onions, finely chopped,
including green part

2 teaspoons each: fresh thyme
leaves, salt

1 to 2 teaspoons ground allspice

1 teaspoon ground black pepper

1/2 teaspoon cinnamon

1/4 teaspoon grated nutmeg

4 to 6 habanero or other chilies,
finely chopped

1 top sirloin, round or flank steak,
about 2 pounds

1. Mix together all ingredients except steak in a food processor or blender, or chop fine by hand.

2. Wearing clean rubber gloves, rub some of the jerk mixture all over the steak. Marinate meat for 10 minutes or as long as an hour. (Leftover jerk seasoning can be refrigerated in a jar for as long as one month.)

3. Grill over medium fire to desired doneness depending on your taste and the cut of meat, about 15 to 20 minutes, turning occasionally.

Barbecuing need not be limited to beef and pork.
Lusciously tender lamb chops adapt equally well to the grill.

Preparation time: 10 minutes
Marinating time: 1 hour
Cooking time: 12 minutes
Yield: 4 servings

---

1 tablespoon coarsely ground black pepper

1 teaspoon each: dried thyme, sweet paprika

$^3/_4$ teaspoon salt

Pinch each: cayenne pepper, ground cumin

4 large or 8 small lamb chops

1. Combine the pepper, thyme, paprika, salt, cayenne and cumin in a small dish. Rub over the chops. Arrange chops in a shallow glass dish and marinate 1 hour.

2. Grill the chops over a hot fire, turning several times, just until cooked to rare or medium-rare. Timing depends on the size of the chops: Small ones will take about 8 minutes, larger ones about 12 minutes.

*A covered grill, a generous amount of charcoal and a bit of careful attention
ensure that this rich, succulent leg of lamb is perfectly cooked and kissed with
the smoky taste of summer.*

Preparation time: 15 minutes
Cooking time: 1^1/2 hours
Yield: 10 servings

**1 whole leg of lamb, trimmed,
about 5 pounds**

2 tablespoons olive or vegetable oil

4 large cloves garlic, minced

^{1}/2 cup fresh mint leaves

^{1}/3 cup fresh cilantro leaves

**2 tablespoons each: fresh oregano,
fresh marjoram**

**1 teaspoon coarsely cracked black
pepper**

**^{1}/2 teaspoon crushed red pepper
flakes**

2 tablespoons Dijon mustard

1. Rub the lamb with the oil. Cut one of the garlic cloves in half and rub it over the meat.

2. Arrange hot coals around the edges of the grill and place a drip pan in the center. Place the lamb on the grate over the drip pan, cover and leave the vents open. Grill for about 15 minutes per pound, or slightly longer, for rare. An instant-read thermometer should read 140 to 145 degrees. The meat will continue to cook after it is removed from the grill.

3. Meanwhile, roughly chop the remaining garlic, herbs, black pepper and red pepper in a food processor or by hand. About 30 minutes before the meat is done, brush the mustard over the top of the lamb and sprinkle with the herb mixture. When it is cooked as desired, transfer the lamb to a heated platter and let stand for 10 minutes before carving.

POULTRY

With the help of the microwave oven, this makes a quick yet elegant grilled entree with an Italian accent.

Preparation time: 15 minutes
Microwave cooking time: 18 to
   23 minutes
Cooking time: 10 minutes
Yield: 4 servings

---

6 tablespoons olive oil

3 tablespoons each: fresh lemon juice, dry red wine

3 sprigs fresh rosemary, chopped, or 1$^1/_4$ teaspoons dried rosemary

Salt, freshly ground black pepper

4 Cornish game hens

2 cloves garlic, halved

1 teaspoon cracked black peppercorns

2 small red onions, halved

2 teaspoons balsamic vinegar

1. Whisk olive oil, lemon juice, wine, a third of the rosemary, $^1/_4$ teaspoon salt and $^1/_8$ teaspoon ground black pepper in 13-by-9-inch glass baking dish.

2. Rinse hens under cold water; pat dry. Rub the cavity of each bird with equal portions of the remaining rosemary, garlic and salt and ground pepper to taste. Truss birds with string, if you like.

3. Align hens in casserole, breast side down. Cover with plastic wrap, vented at one corner. Microwave on high (100 percent power) 5 to 7 minutes. Rotate hens, placing the two outer ones in the center positions. Re-cover and microwave on high 3 to 4 minutes. Turn breast side up. Sprinkle with cracked pepper. Add onions to casserole. Cover with plastic wrap. Microwave on high until juices run clear, 10 to 12 minutes, rotating hens once. Let stand 5 minutes to finish cooking.

4. Grill hens breast side down in a covered grill over medium-hot coals for 5 minutes. Turn breast side up and brush lightly with vinegar. Place onions on grill, cut side down. Grill, uncovered, until skin of hens is fairly crisp and brown, about 5 minutes. Serve hot or at room temperature.

GAME HENS WITH LIME

The simplicity of this recipe makes it the perfect choice for those who are watching their fat and calorie intake. This recipe would also work well with small chickens. Serve with plenty of vegetables and a grain dish.

Preparation time: 10 minutes
Cooking time: 45 minutes
Yield: 2 to 4 servings

---

2 Cornish game hens

Freshly ground black pepper

3 limes

$^1/_2$ cup each: fresh lime juice, low-sodium chicken broth

1. Season the hens inside and out with pepper. Cut 2 of the limes in half; put 2 halves inside the cavity of each hen. Truss hens.

2. Mix lime juice and chicken broth in bowl. Brush over hens.

3. Grill hens in a covered grill over a medium fire until juices run clear, 40 to 45 minutes. Brush occasionally with lime juice mixture. Cut third lime into wedges for garnish.

Food writer Pat Dailey suggests a delicious way to enjoy grilled chicken that involves just a little preparation beforehand.

Preparation time: 20 minutes
Marinating time: 4 hours or
  overnight
Cooking time: 30 minutes
Yield: 4 servings

$^1/_2$ cup vegetable oil

$^1/_3$ cup orange juice

$^1/_4$ cup red wine vinegar

1 tablespoon Dijon mustard

1 teaspoon each: salt, cayenne pepper, crushed mustard seeds

4 small frying chickens, cut in half

1. Combine the oil, orange juice, vinegar, mustard, salt, cayenne and mustard seeds in a small bowl. Transfer to a shallow glass dish and add the chicken. Cover and refrigerate 4 hours or overnight. Remove chicken from marinade; reserve marinade.

2. Push hot coals to two sides of the grill, leaving the center empty. Arrange chicken over the center area of the grill and brush with marinade. Cover and cook until juices run clear, 20 to 30 minutes, turning and basting the chicken occasionally. Serve hot or at room temperature.

Food and wine columnist William Rice discovered a most unique recipe for grilled poultry for the holiday season. It is based on one from Shaun Hill, a cook at Gidleigh Park, an English country-house hotel. Pheasant or Cornish hens can be used if you can't find guinea hens through a specialty food shop or butcher.

Preparation time: 25 minutes
Cooking time: 55 minutes
Yield: 4 servings

---

2 guinea hens, about 2³/4 pounds each

Peanut oil

12 pearl onions, peeled

12 small carrots, peeled

2 slices thick-cut bacon

¹/2 teaspoon ground mace

Salt, freshly ground black pepper

¹/4 cup each: tomato puree, dry red wine

1 cup cold water

8 peeled chestnuts (see note)

1 sprig fresh thyme

Black truffle slivers, optional

1. Carefully remove the breast meat from the hens. Lightly pound the breasts between sheets of waxed paper to a uniform thickness. Coat the breasts with a light film of oil; cover and refrigerate.

2. Cut the legs off the birds; cut the hens in two with a cleaver or sharp knife.

3. Heat a heavy casserole. Fry the carcasses and legs, onions, carrots and bacon in 2 tablespoons oil until they start to color. Add mace, salt and pepper, then stir in the tomato puree and wine. Add water; heat to a boil.

4. Cut the chestnuts into quarters; add to the casserole along with the thyme. Cover and cook over low heat for 30 minutes. Remove vegetables and chestnuts and put into a small saucepan. Remove cooked meat from bones and add to saucepan; strain the cooking juices over them.

5. Season the breasts with salt and pepper; grill over medium-hot fire until just cooked through, 7 to 10 minutes. Remove the skin before serving, if desired. Serve the breasts atop the braised chestnuts, meat and vegetables. Garnish with truffles, if desired.

Note: Peeled chestnuts are available in vacuum packs at specialty food shops.

It's faster than traditional oven roasting, it frees up the oven for all the other things that need to be baked and, most importantly, the meat becomes infused with a gentle smoky taste. Here, the turkey is flavored with a spicy rub, which also can be used on whole turkey breast.

Preparation time: 5 minutes
Cooking time: About 3 hours
Yield (15-pound turkey):
   12 to 15 servings

1/4 cup each: coarse (kosher) salt, dark brown sugar

4 cloves garlic, minced

2 tablespoons minced yellow onion

4 teaspoons crushed black peppercorns

2 teaspoons crushed red pepper flakes

1 teaspoon ground ginger

1/2 teaspoon each, ground: cloves, allspice

1 turkey, about 15 pounds, thawed in refrigerator if frozen

Vegetable oil

1. Mix all the ingredients except the turkey and oil in small bowl.

2. Remove the giblets from the turkey. Rinse the bird inside and out with cold water; drain well and pat dry with paper towels.

3. Thoroughly rub spice mixture over surface of bird and into cavities. Refrigerate turkey, well wrapped in a plastic bag, at least 6 hours or up to 2 days.

4. Before cooking, rinse turkey thoroughly; pat dry. Rub all over with a light film of oil.

5. Prepare the coals to cook by the indirect method, using about 30 briquets on each side of the grill (or a few more if it is very cold outside). Fit a drip pan between the two rows of coals in the bottom of the grill. When the coals are white, place the turkey on the grill, breast side up.

6. Cover the grill. Cook the turkey for 10 to 13 minutes per pound, opening the grill as seldom as possible. The internal temperature of the thigh area should read 175 to 180 degrees. Transfer the turkey to a large platter and tent it with aluminum foil. Let stand 10 minutes before carving.

This skewered chicken, served hot or cold as an appetizer, delivers tartness tempered with an alluring peanut flavor. Once you assemble the ingredients, the rest is easy.

Preparation time: 25 minutes
Marinating time: 1 hour
Cooking time: 6 minutes
Yield: 4 to 6 servings

---

3 large whole chicken breasts, boned, skinned, split

1 small onion, cut in half

¹/₃ cup unsalted, dry-roasted peanuts

3 tablespoons fresh cilantro leaves

3 large cloves garlic

1 piece (¹/₂-inch) fresh ginger

2 tablespoons each: vegetable oil, fish sauce (nam pla, see note)

2 tablespoons each: chicken broth, fresh lime juice

2 teaspoons each: red wine vinegar, sugar

¹/₄ teaspoon salt

1. Cut each breast half into 6 equal pieces. Put chicken into large plastic food bag.

2. Put onion, peanuts, cilantro, garlic and ginger into blender or food processor; process until smooth. Add oil, fish sauce, chicken broth, lime juice, vinegar, sugar and salt. Mix well. Add to chicken. Seal bag and refrigerate 1 hour.

3. Remove chicken from marinade. Thread 4 pieces of chicken on wooden or metal skewers, leaving a slight space between each piece. (If you're using wooden skewers, soak them in cold water for 20 minutes before using.) Grill over hot fire, turning once, just until no longer pink, 2 to 3 minutes each side. Serve hot or at room temperature.

Note: Fish sauce is available at Thai and other Asian markets. Nuoc nam can be substituted.

*If you want something different and impressive, but not too difficult to make,
this simple chicken dish is it.
Serve with roasted or grilled vegetables and sauteed spinach.*

Preparation time: 15 minutes
Marinating time: 30 to 60 minutes
Cooking time: 10 minutes
Yield: 12 servings

---

1 cup prepared pesto sauce

2 tablespoons seasoned rice vinegar

1 tablespoon Dijon mustard

1 teaspoon coarse ground black pepper

$^1/_8$ teaspoon cayenne pepper

6 large whole chicken breasts, boned, split

1. Combine the pesto sauce, vinegar, mustard, black pepper and cayenne pepper in a small bowl. Transfer to a large plastic food bag and add chicken. Seal the bag tightly and turn it over several times so chicken is well coated. Refrigerate 30 to 60 minutes.

2. Remove chicken from marinade. Grill over medium-hot fire, turning once, until cooked, about 10 minutes.

The incredible persistence of the Caesar salad in American cuisine has made it a true classic — but one that certainly can tolerate a little innovation. At the Eccentric Restaurant in Chicago they often add grilled chicken to make it a main course.

Preparation time: 30 minutes
Marinating time: 30 minutes
Cooking time: 10 minutes
Yield: 4 servings

CHICKEN

2 whole chicken breasts, split, skinned, boned

$^1/_2$ cup vegetable oil

1 tablespoon paprika

2 teaspoons crushed garlic

SALAD

1 clove garlic

3 or 4 anchovies, patted dry

$1^1/_2$ tablespoons fresh lemon juice

$1^1/_4$ tablespoons red wine vinegar

$1^1/_2$ teaspoons cold water

1 large egg yolk (see note)

$1^1/_2$ teaspoons Dijon mustard

1 cup olive oil

2 tablespoons hot water

$^3/_4$ cup (3 ounces) grated Parmesan cheese

2 small heads romaine lettuce, washed, crisped

Freshly ground pepper

$^3/_4$ cup croutons

Grated Parmesan cheese for topping

1. For the chicken, combine the oil, paprika and garlic in shallow dish. Add chicken; turn to coat and marinate in the refrigerator at least 30 minutes.

2. For salad, mince garlic in food processor or blender. Add anchovies, lemon juice, vinegar and cold water; mix thoroughly. Whisk egg yolk and mustard together in mixing bowl. Slowly whisk in pureed anchovy mixture, then olive oil. When all oil is added, add hot water and cheese.

3. Remove chicken from marinade and pat dry. Grill over medium-hot fire, turning once, until cooked, about 10 minutes. Cut crosswise into strips and keep warm.

4. Tear lettuce into bite-size pieces in large bowl. Toss with dressing to taste. Divide among 4 large chilled plates and sprinkle with freshly ground pepper. Arrange chicken over top and sprinkle with croutons and cheese.

Note: If you prefer not to use raw egg yolk in the dressing, you may substitute 2 tablespoons whipping cream.

TARRAGON CHICKEN SANDWICHES

If sandwiches once were reserved for lunch boxes and family-only suppers, those rules no longer apply, says food writer Pat Dailey. Now, sandwiches often serve as party food, such as these chicken breasts, bathed in a summery sauce and grilled, then layered with cheese and tomatoes. Also try adding red onions, grilled summer squash and grilled eggplant.

Preparation time: 30 minutes
Marinating time: 30 minutes
Cooking time: 8 to 10 minutes
Yield: 4 servings

---

1 small clove garlic

$^1/_3$ cup fresh tarragon leaves

$1^1/_2$ ounces fontinella cheese plus 4 slices

2 tablespoons walnut halves

$^1/_2$ cup extra-virgin olive oil

$^1/_4$ teaspoon salt

2 whole chicken breasts, boned, skinned, split

4 egg twist rolls, split

4 tomato slices

1. Mince the garlic, tarragon, $1^1/_2$ ounces cheese and walnuts in a food processor or blender. Add the oil and salt; mix well.

2. Transfer half of the mixure to a large plastic food bag and add the chicken. Seal tightly and refrigerate at least 30 minutes. Reserve the remaining mixture.

3. Grill the chicken over medium-hot fire, turning once, until cooked, 8 to 10 minutes. Shortly before the chicken is cooked, place the rolls at the edges of the grill and cook until lightly toasted.

4. To assemble the sandwiches, brush some of the remaining tarragon mixture inside the rolls. Put chicken on each roll bottom; add a slice of cheese and a slice of tomato and cover with top of roll. Serve hot or at room temperature.

Boneless duck breasts, with or without the skin, are available at many markets, making duck as easy an option as chicken. Here, the breasts are marinated in a sweet/tart mixture that also is used to sauce them. They're cooked with the skin on so they stay juicy and flavorful; the skin can be removed after cooking if desired.

Preparation time: 10 minutes
Marinating time: 1 to 2 hours
Cooking time: 10 minutes
Yield: 4 servings

$^1/_2$ **cup each: fresh lime juice, chicken broth, Riesling wine**

$^1/_4$ **cup seasoned rice vinegar**

2 tablespoons mango chutney, such as Major Grey's

1 tablespoon minced fresh ginger

2 whole boneless duck breasts

2 tablespoons unsalted butter

1. In a food processor or blender, mix together the lime juice, chicken broth, wine, vinegar, chutney and ginger. Transfer half of the mixture to a shallow glass dish. Add the duck and turn it over so it is coated with marinade. Cover and refrigerate 1 to 2 hours.

2. Meanwhile, transfer the other half of the mixture to a small non-aluminum saucepan. Boil, uncovered, until it is reduced to $^1/_2$ cup, about 5 minutes. Set aside.

3. Grill the duck over a medium-hot fire, turning once, just until it is pink in the center, 7 to 10 minutes. Transfer to a warm platter and tent with aluminum foil while you finish the sauce.

4. Bring the sauce mixture back to a boil. Reduce the heat to low and whisk in one tablespoon of the butter, whisking constantly and waiting until it is melted before whisking in the other. Serve the duck with sauce on the side.

FISH AND SEAFOOD

*Once called the poor man's lobster, monkfish has earned the right
to be recognized on its own merits.
Here it stars on the grill in a recipe inspired by Mexican cooks.*

Preparation time: 20 minutes
Marinating time: 2 hours
Cooking time: 7 minutes
Yield: 4 to 6 servings

---

1 orange

3 tablespoons each: light olive oil, chopped fresh cilantro

1 tablespoon soy sauce

2 cloves garlic, minced

1 serrano chili, minced

2 teaspoons fresh lime juice

1 teaspoon finely chopped fresh ginger

$1/4$ teaspoon ground cumin

2 pounds monkfish fillets, cut into $3/4$-inch chunks, rinsed, patted dry

Lemon or orange slices for serving

1. Grate rind of orange into large bowl. Squeeze 1 tablespoon of the juice and add to bowl along with oil, 2 tablespoons of the cilantro, soy sauce, garlic, chili, lime juice, ginger and cumin. Add fish and stir well. Cover and refrigerate for at least 2 hours, turning several times.

2. Put fish onto 4 or 6 metal or wooden skewers. (If using wooden skewers, first soak in water 20 minutes.) Grill fish over a medium-hot fire, turning once, until fish is opaque, 5 to 6 minutes. Garnish with remaining cilantro and lemon or orange slices.

Whether you select steaks or fillets, salmon is a terrific choice for the grill. With its own distinctive taste, it can be grilled plain and topped with a simple relish. But it also is well enhanced by myriad ethnic flavors, such as the robust Asian ingredients in this marinade.

Preparation time: 20 minutes
Marinating time: 30 minutes
  or longer
Cooking time: 10 minutes
Yield: 4 servings

---

1 piece fresh ginger, about 1-inch cube

1 teaspoon grated lemon rind

3 tablespoons lemon juice

2 tablespoons each: vegetable oil, honey

2 teaspoons each: grainy mustard, soy sauce

$^1/_2$ teaspoon salt

4 salmon fillets or steaks, 6 to 7 ounces each

1. Combine the ginger, lemon rind, lemon juice, oil, honey, mustard, soy sauce and salt in a blender; mix until smooth.

2. Arrange fish in a shallow glass dish and pour marinade over it. Turn the fish several times so it is well coated; cover and refrigerate 30 minutes or longer.

3. Remove salmon from marinade, letting excess drip off. Lightly brush grill with vegetable oil. Grill fish over a hot fire, turning once, until it is just cooked in the center, 6 to 10 minutes.

The short season for soft-shell crab makes it a treat to anticipate and savor. This Tex/Mex extravaganza, based on an idea from Gordon Sinclair of Chicago's Gordon restaurant, combines the crab with tortillas, black beans and traditional taco garnishes. Many of the ingredients can be prepared in advance.

Preparation time: 35 minutes
Cooking time: 5 minutes
Yield: 2 servings

BLACK BEAN PUREE

1 cup canned or cooked dried black beans

1/2 cup each: chopped green and red bell pepper

1 small onion, chopped

1 jalapeno chili, seeded if desired

2 tablespoons vegetable oil

1 to 2 tablespoons white wine vinegar

1 tablespoon chopped cilantro

1 teaspoon ground cumin

Salt, pepper to taste

CILANTRO CREAM

1 bunch fresh cilantro

1 cup sour cream

Salt, white pepper to taste

CRABS

4 soft-shell crabs, cleaned

2 tablespoons vegetable oil

FOR SERVING

4 corn tortillas

Salsa, guacamole, lime wedges, cilantro sprigs

1. For the puree, combine all ingredients in a food processor or blender; mix until finely chopped but not fully pureed. Set aside. Can be made a day ahead and refrigerated.

2. For cilantro cream, put cilantro leaves in a medium strainer. Immerse in boiling water for 5 seconds; immediately plunge into ice water. Drain well and pat dry. Puree in a food processor or blender with the sour cream, and salt and pepper to taste. Set aside.

3. Brush the crabs and tortillas with oil. Grill the crabs over a medium-hot fire, turning once, just until they are cooked, 3 to 5 minutes. Just before the crabs are finished, put the tortillas on the grill to warm them.

4. To serve, spread black bean mixture over tortillas. Arrange 1 or 2 crabs over beans and spoon salsa, guacamole and cilantro cream around edges. Garnish with lime and cilantro sprigs.

Tuna, fresh from the fish counter or market, is a meaty, healthful source of protein that adapts well to the grill. Food and wine columnist William Rice suggests this Asian treatment. Despite a trend toward serving tuna barely warm and almost raw in the center, Rice suggests that a little more cooking will render the best results.

Preparation time: 20 minutes
Standing time: 20 minutes
Cooking time: 5 minutes
Yield: 4 servings

---

4 tuna steaks, about 6 ounces each, cut ¹/₂ inch thick

¹/₄ cup minced green onion

2 cloves garlic, minced

¹/₂ teaspoon each: dry mustard, cornstarch, ground black pepper

¹/₄ teaspoon ground star anise

2 tablespoons sesame oil

Salt or soy sauce to taste

1. Bring tuna steaks to room temperature while preparing coating. Make a paste by mixing the green onion, garlic, mustard, cornstarch, pepper, star anise and sesame oil. Spread on both sides of the tuna. With a small knife, coat the edges with the coating as well. Let stand for 20 minutes.

2. Grill over a hot fire, turning once, until the fish is cooked medium-rare, about 5 minutes. It should be pink in the center but warm all the way through. Season with salt or soy sauce after turning.

SKEWERED SHRIMP AND SCALLOPS WITH CREAMY HERBED MARINADE

Shrimp and scallops are just the right size for tandem barbecuing on skewers. The mayonnaise base of this summery marinade helps seal in the juices, giving an extra measure of protection against their tendency to dry out. The marinade also works with other fish, chicken and beef.

Preparation time: 20 minutes
Marinating time: 3 hours
Cooking time: 4 to 6 minutes
Yield: 4 servings

$1/2$ cup mayonnaise

2 large green onions, minced

2 teaspoons fresh lemon juice

1 teaspoon each: Creole or coarse French mustard, Worcestershire sauce

2 teaspoons minced fresh basil or $1/2$ teaspoon dried

1 teaspoon minced fresh rosemary or $1/4$ teaspoon dried

1 teaspoon minced fresh oregano or $1/4$ teaspoon dried

$1/2$ teaspoon each: paprika, freshly ground black pepper

$1/4$ teaspoon kosher salt

$1/8$ to $1/4$ teaspoon cayenne

1 pound medium or large shrimp, shelled, deveined

$3/4$ pound sea scallops

1. Whisk mayonnaise, green onions, lemon juice, mustard, Worcestershire sauce, herbs, paprika, pepper, salt and cayenne together in medium bowl. Adjust spiciness to taste.

2. Pat shrimp and scallops dry. Add to marinade; gently toss. Cover and refrigerate about 3 hours.

3. Alternate shrimp and scallops on wooden or metal skewers. (If using wooden skewers, first soak in water 20 minutes.) Reserve any remaining marinade.

4. Grill over a medium-hot fire until shrimp and scallops are opaque, 4 to 6 minutes, turning every 2 minutes and brushing with reserved marinade several times.

Cool Greek flavors and a lovely wash of colors make this a most inviting summertime preparation.

Preparation time: 20 minutes
Marinating time: 1 hour or more
Cooking time: 30 minutes
Yield: 4 servings

---

8 to 12 baby artichokes (see note)

$1/2$ cup olive oil

$1/4$ cup fresh lemon juice

1 clove garlic, minced

1 teaspoon each: dried oregano, Dijon mustard

$1/2$ teaspoon dried rosemary

$1/4$ to $1/2$ teaspoon crushed red pepper flakes

Salt, freshly ground black pepper

16 jumbo shrimp, peeled, tail left intact

1 lemon

1. Cook artichokes in boiling salted water just until tender, 8 to 12 minutes, depending on their size. Drain well and hold under cold running water until they are cool to the touch. Artichokes can be cooked a day in advance and refrigerated.

2. Combine oil, lemon juice, garlic, oregano, mustard, rosemary, red pepper flakes, salt and pepper in a large plastic food bag. Add shrimp, seal tightly and refrigerate 1 hour or longer before cooking.

3. If artichokes are very small, leave them whole. Larger ones should be cut in half lengthwise and the choke removed. Trim pointed tips of leaves if they are sharp. Thread artichokes and shrimp alternately onto 4 metal or wooden skewers. (If using wooden skewers, first soak in water 20 minutes.) Brush with any remaining marinade.

4. Grill brochettes over a hot fire, turning once, until shrimp is cooked through, 7 to 9 minutes. Garnish with lemon wedges.

Note: Baby artichokes, about 2 inches long, are too young to have developed the prickly inside choke, so the entire artichoke can be eaten. If baby artichokes are not available, use the smallest mature ones you can find. Cook until they are just tender, then cut in half lengthwise and remove the choke.

Swordfish has a special affinity for the grill. Its meaty texture is perfectly served by the open flame, and a mix of charcoal and hardwood adds a delicious taste. Serve these steaks hot or at room temperature.

Preparation time: 20 minutes
Cooking time: 8 minutes
Yield: 4 servings

---

1 cucumber

1 small hot red pepper

$^1/_2$ small onion

3 tablespoons each: seasoned rice vinegar, minced fresh cilantro

1 tablespoon minced fresh mint

4 swordfish steaks, about 1 inch thick

1. Split the cucumber in half lengthwise; scrape out seeds from the center. Dice the unpeeled cucumber, red pepper and onion into very small pieces. Combine in a bowl with the vinegar and herbs.

2. Brush the grill with a small amount of vegetable oil. Grill the fish over a hot fire, turning once, until it is cooked through, about 8 minutes. Serve with the relish spooned over the top.

For many tastes, red snapper is the premier ocean fish, distinguished by its delicate, sweet taste and fine texture. One classic preparation combines whole snapper with a colorful Mexican sauce that has a play of hot, tart and salty tastes.

Preparation time: 30 minutes
Cooking time: 10 to 15 minutes
Yield: 3 to 4 servings

---

1 small each, diced: red and yellow bell pepper

1 small red onion, finely diced

1 hot chili pepper, preferably red, cut in thin rings

1 large tomato, seeded, diced

3 tomatillos, diced (optional)

8 green olives, preferably oil-cured, pitted, halved

$1/4$ cup chopped fresh cilantro

3 tablespoons olive oil

2 to 3 tablespoons fresh lime juice

Salt, freshly ground pepper

1 whole red snapper, about 4 pounds, cleaned, dressed

Cilantro for garnish

1. Combine the bell peppers, onion, chili, tomatoes, tomatillos, olives and cilantro in a bowl. Toss with the oil and lime juice, and salt and pepper to taste.

2. Brush a grill basket or the grill with oil. Grill the snapper over a medium-hot fire, turning once, for about 10 minutes per inch of thickness. Spoon the sauce over a large heated platter and carefully place the whole fish over. Garnish with additional cilantro.

The heady scent of a charcoal fire is easily matched by the haunting aroma of the Middle Eastern spices used here. Hummus dip, grilled eggplant and pita bread round out a fine feast.

Preparation time: 25 minutes
Cooking time: 10 minutes
Yield: 4 servings

---

3 tablespoons olive oil

1 teaspoon ground turmeric

1/2 teaspoon ground cumin

1/4 teaspoon each: cinnamon, ground coriander

1 very large sweet onion, diced

1 cup chopped walnuts

3 tablespoons dried currants

Salt, cayenne pepper, freshly ground black pepper

4 whole brook or rainbow trout, about 1/2 pound each, cleaned, dressed

Lime wedges, cilantro for garnish

1. Heat the oil in a medium saucepan. Stir in the spices and onions. Cook gently, stirring occasionally, until onions are limp but not browned, 12 to 15 minutes. Remove from heat and add the walnuts and currants. Add salt, cayenne and black pepper to taste.

2. Pat the fish dry. Brush the grill or a grill basket lightly with vegetable oil. Grill over a medium-hot fire, turning once, until fish is cooked, 8 to 10 minutes. Squeeze fresh lime juice over the fish and garnish with cilantro. Serve with the onion relish.

GO-WITHS

Vegetables should be grilled over high but not scorching heat, which is efficient because you can grill them while waiting for the charcoal to get hot enough for steak or fish. Many varieties of vegetables are appropriate for this dish, so select your favorites.

Preparation time: 30 minutes
Cooking time: 1 hour
Yield: 4 to 6 servings

$^2/_3$ cup (approximately) extra-virgin olive oil

2 cloves garlic, unpeeled

1 each: yellow squash, zucchini, yellow and red onions, red and green bell peppers

10 medium mushrooms

2 small fennel bulbs, trimmed

4 to 6 baby artichokes, trimmed

4 to 6 slender carrots, scrubbed

2 to 3 small leeks, cleaned

2 to 4 tablespoons balsamic vinegar

8 sun-dried tomatoes

1 cup imported black olives

2 tablespoons drained capers

French or Italian bread for serving

1. Heat oven to 300 degrees. Put 3 tablespoons of the oil with the garlic in two large layers of aluminum foil; wrap tightly. Bake until garlic is tender but not burned, 30 to 40 minutes. When cool enough to touch, squeeze the garlic from its skin and mix with the oil in which it was cooked to make a paste. Set aside. (This can be done up to several hours in advance.)

2. Brush or rub the vegetables with some of the oil. Season lightly with salt and pepper. Grill over a hot fire, turning as necessary, until tender yet still slightly crisp.

3. Transfer the vegetables to a large bowl and toss them in the vinegar and 5 tablespoons of the oil. Arrange them on a platter along with the sun-dried tomatoes, olives and capers.

4. Cut the bread into thick slices. Grill lightly over a medium fire. (Or, use the oven to toast the bread.) Spread with the garlic paste. Serve with the vegetables.

Sparking up that traditional barbecue side dish, cole slaw, is simply a matter of using red cabbage, carrots, and red, green and yellow peppers, according to Chicago Tribune columnist Abby Mandel. The result? A riot of color and a great-tasting salad.

Preparation time: 25 minutes
Yield: 6 servings

---

1 medium head red cabbage, thinly sliced

1 each, roasted, cut in strips: red, green and yellow bell pepper

3 large carrots, julienned

5 tablespoons balsamic vinegar

3 tablespoons olive oil

1 teaspoon coarse ground black pepper

$^3/_4$ teaspoon salt

$^1/_2$ teaspoon each: celery seed, dried oregano, dried basil, sugar

Mix the cabbage, bell peppers and carrots in a large bowl. In a smaller bowl, combine the remaining ingredients. Add to the cabbage and mix well. Slaw can be served immediately or refrigerated overnight. Mix well and adjust the seasoning before serving.

Call this recipe a salad or call it a relish. As a relish, it can be used to top simple grilled fish entrees or served with tortilla chips. Spooned into lettuce cups or avocado halves, it makes a nice, light warm-weather meal.

Preparation time: 25 minutes
Yield: About 2 cups

---

2 ounces lean slab bacon, finely diced

1 small each, diced: roasted red and green bell pepper

1 large green onion, thinly sliced

1 small jalapeno chili, minced

1 can (15 to 16 ounces) black beans, drained

3 tablespoons minced fresh cilantro

2 tablespoons olive oil

1 tablespoon each: fresh orange juice, fresh lime juice, tequila

Salt to taste

Fry the bacon until crisp. Drain well and combine with remaining ingredients. Let stand at least 10 minutes before serving.

On a hot grill, pizza crust is seared almost instantly, taking on a nice smoky taste. In fact, the grill is about as close as a home cook will get to replicating the aroma and taste of fancy restaurant pizzas cooked in wood-burning ovens.

Preparation time: 30 minutes
Rising time: 1 hour
Cooking time: 15 minutes
Yield: 6 8-inch pizzas

CRUST

1 package active dry yeast

1 teaspoon sugar

1 cup warm water (105 to 115 degrees)

3 cups unbleached all-purpose flour

1 teaspoon salt

2 tablespoons olive oil

PIZZA

1 small each: red and yellow bell pepper

1 sweet onion, quartered

Olive oil

4 ounces spicy sausage (such as andouille or Italian)

1¹/₂ cups (6 ounces) shredded mozzarella cheese

¹/₂ cup (2 ounces) grated Parmesan cheese

Snipped fresh basil, salt, crushed red pepper flakes to taste

1. Stir yeast and sugar into warm water; let stand 5 minutes or until foamy. Combine flour and salt in a food processor with the metal blade or in a mixing bowl. Add the yeast mixture and mix until a soft but not sticky dough forms. If dough is too dry, add additional water by the teaspoonful. Mix in olive oil.

2. Knead dough until smooth and elastic, about 45 seconds in the processor, 7 to 8 minutes by hand. Place in an oiled bowl, cover and let rise until doubled, about 1 hour. Dough can be used immediately or punched down, covered tightly and refrigerated overnight.

3. Divide dough into 6 pieces. Roll each into an 8-inch circle. The pizzas can be cooked immediately, or the rolled dough can be stacked between sheets of aluminum foil and refrigerated for up to 2 days.

4. Brush the peppers and onion with oil. Grill the vegetables and sausage over a hot fire until cooked through, 5 to 10 minutes. Cut peppers and onion into strips. Slice sausage.

5. Brush one side of the rolled crusts with olive oil. Place on grill, oiled side down. Grill until set, 3 to 4 minutes. Turn and brush with oil. Sprinkle with mozzarella cheese, then add the peppers, onion and sausage. Top with Parmesan, basil, salt and pepper flakes. Drizzle oil over all. Grill, covered, until crust is cooked and cheese is melted, 3 to 4 minutes.

Nothing delivers Tex-Mex flavors as well as salsa, and this red-pepper variety from Chicago Tribune *food columnist Abby Mandel makes a classic. The fresher the ingredients, the better it tastes.*

Preparation time: 15 minutes
Yield: About 1 1/2 cups

---

1 cup fresh cilantro

1 jalapeno or serrano chili, seeded if desired

1 small each, quartered: onion, red bell pepper

2 medium tomatoes, quartered, seeded

1 1/2 teaspoons red or white wine vinegar

1/4 teaspoon salt

1. Put cilantro in the work bowl of a food processor; turn on the machine and drop the chili through the feed tube to mince. Add onion and red pepper to bowl and mince roughly. Add tomatoes, vinegar and salt and process just until tomatoes are coarsely chopped. Be sure to retain some texture. (Or to make by hand, mince the cilantro, chili, onion, red pepper and tomatoes; mix with the vinegar and salt.)

2. This is best served the day it is made, but it can be refrigerated overnight. Drain the liquid and adjust the seasoning before serving. Serve with tortilla chips or as a table condiment.

Bruschetta is simply an Italian word for sliced bread that is rubbed with raw garlic, brushed with a fruity olive oil, then grilled. Top it with a tomato, olive and basil salad for a succulent side dish or a wonderful summer lunch.

Preparation time: 20 minutes
Cooking time: 5 minutes
Yield: 8 servings

BREAD

1 loaf French bread, about 1 pound, 16 inches long

1 large clove garlic, split

About $1/4$ cup olive oil

SALAD

4 large ripe tomatoes, seeded, chopped

14 kalamata olives, halved, pitted

$1/3$ cup julienned fresh basil leaves

$1/4$ cup each: balsamic vinegar, olive oil, minced onion

$1/2$ teaspoon salt

$1/4$ teaspoon sugar

Freshly ground black pepper

Basil leaves for garnish

1. For bread, split loaf horizontally in half. Grill, cut side down, over medium-hot fire until the bread is lightly toasted.

2. Rub toasted side with the split garlic clove. Brush with olive oil. Cut each half of bread crosswise into four equal portions, for a total of eight pieces.

3. For the salad, mix the tomatoes, olives, basil, vinegar, oil, onion, salt, sugar and pepper in 1-quart bowl. Use immediately or let stand at room temperature as long as 2 hours. Adjust seasoning.

4. To serve, arrange bread on a serving plate. Using a slotted spoon, place heaping portions of the salad on each slice of bread. Drizzle remaining dressing in bowl over the top. Garnish with basil leaves. Serve immediately.

*Whether you eat it with a fork or wrap it in a warm tortilla,
this spicy salad from* Chicago Tribune *columnist Abby Mandel complements
many kinds of barbecued meats, especially poultry. If you use tortillas,
keep them warm by wrapping them in foil or in a cloth napkin.
That also keeps them soft enough to roll without breaking.*

Preparation time: 30 minutes
Yield: 8 servings

DRESSING

^{1}/3 cup fresh lime juice

2 tablespoons mild red or green pepper jelly

1 tablespoon each: water, vegetable oil

SALAD

1 large zucchini, diced into ^{1}/2-inch pieces

^{1}/2 cup corn kernels, fresh, frozen or canned, well drained

5 large green onions, thinly sliced

1 large red bell pepper, diced into ^{1}/2-inch pieces

^{1}/2 small jicama, peeled, diced into ^{1}/2-inch pieces

^{1}/3 cup chunky fresh salsa, well drained

^{1}/3 cup fresh cilantro leaves, chopped

Salt to taste

^{1}/2 large head iceberg lettuce, thinly sliced

16 flour tortillas (6-inch), warmed, optional

Cilantro sprigs, lime quarters

1. For dressing, combine all ingredients in a small pan or a microwave-safe bowl. Warm on the stove or in microwave oven until jelly melts. Stir to combine. Can be made 2 days ahead and refrigerated.

2. For salad, combine zucchini, corn, green onions, bell pepper, jicama, salsa and cilantro in a 1^1/2-quart mixing bowl. Toss with dressing and add salt to taste. Can be made a day ahead and refrigerated. Stir well before using, then drain all liquid.

3. To serve, arrange lettuce on serving platter. Spoon salad over lettuce. Garnish platter with cilantro sprigs and lime wedges. Serve spooned onto tortillas, if desired.

This recipe was served at Goodfellow's restaurant in Minneapolis, right in the heart of wild rice country. Good hot or cold, it is a fine companion to grilled poultry or pork.

Preparation time: 20 minutes
Cooking time: 1 hour
Yield: 3 to 4 servings

1¹/₂ cups wild rice

1 medium ear sweet corn in the husk

2 tablespoons unsalted butter

¹/₄ cup each: diced hickory-smoked ham and hulled sugar snap peas or baby peas

1 tablespoon soy sauce or to taste

Freshly ground pepper

1. Cook rice according to package directions. Grill the corn in the husk over a hot fire until just tender, about 5 minutes. When it is cool enough to handle, cut the corn off the cob.

2. Heat butter in large skillet. When hot, add rice, ham, peas and corn. Cook over medium-high heat until hot, about 2 minutes. Add soy sauce and pepper. Stir well and cook 1 minute. Serve hot or cold.

TARRAGON POTATO SALAD

What goes best with barbecued ribs, or barbecued anything for that matter?
Certainly potato salad is one prime candidate for that honor.
For Chicago Tribune *food and wine columnist William Rice,*
the simpler the better, as his recipe proves.

Preparation time: 40 minutes
Cooking time: 25 minutes
Yield: 6 to 8 servings

---

6 medium red potatoes

¹/₄ cup each: dry white wine, white wine vinegar

¹/₄ teaspoon each: salt, black pepper, paprika

Cayenne pepper to taste

¹/₄ cup finely chopped green onion

2 tablespoons finely chopped fresh tarragon

¹/₃ cup olive oil

²/₃ cup mayonnaise

2 hard-cooked eggs, peeled, chopped

1. Cook the whole, unpeeled potatoes in boiling, salted water until tender but still firm, about 15 minutes depending on size.

2. Meanwhile, combine wine, vinegar, salt, black pepper, paprika, cayenne, onion and 1 tablespoon tarragon in large mixing bowl. Slowly beat in oil.

3. Drain the potatoes. Peel potatoes while still warm, and cut them into small pieces directly into the bowl, tossing with the dressing. Pour in additional wine, vinegar and oil if needed.

4. Add the mayonnaise, chopped eggs and remaining tablespoon of tarragon. Stir in, mashing some of the potato as you do. Taste and adjust seasoning as desired. Set aside for at least half an hour. Do not refrigerate unless there is a long delay before the salad is to be served.

CHILI-LIME CORN IN THE HUSK

While you grill the main course, place corn in the husk next to it to cook. Serve with this spicy butter and the juice from wedges of fresh lime. Of course, the butter can be used on boiled or steamed corn, too.

Preparation time: 20 minutes
Soaking time: 15 minutes
Cooking time: 15 minutes
Yield: 8 ears

$1/2$ cup (1 stick) unsalted butter, softened

2 to 3 teaspoons ground New Mexico chilies

Salt, cayenne pepper

8 ears sweet corn in the husks

8 lime wedges

1. Mix the butter, ground chilies, salt and cayenne pepper until smooth. Butter can be used immediately or wrapped tightly and refrigerated up to one week.

2. Pull the corn husks back from the ears, leaving them attached at the base of the stalk. Remove the silk and pull the husks back up around the ears. Soak corn in cold water for 15 minutes before grilling.

3. Grill the corn over a hot open fire until tender, 10 to 15 minutes, turning several times.

4. Serve the corn with the butter and lime wedges.

Classic, slow-cooked baked beans are not only the pride of Boston but of just about every backyard barbecue and cookout across America. Here, the classic formula is changed, but only slightly. Several varieties of beans are brought together in a sauce of brown sugar, bacon and maple syrup.

Preparation time: 25 minutes
Soaking time: Overnight
Cooking time: 4 hours
Yield: 12 servings

---

1 pound dried beans, preferably a mix of several types such as navy, rattlesnake, pinto and anasazi

8 ounces smoked slab bacon, finely diced

2 medium onions, chopped

1 cup each: packed light brown sugar, ketchup

$1/2$ cup pure maple syrup

2 tablespoons Worcestershire sauce

1 teaspoon dry mustard

1. Soak beans in a generous amount of cold water for 12 hours or overnight. Drain well. Place in a large pot with fresh cold water.

2. Heat to a simmer; cook partially covered until beans are just tender to the bite, 1 to $1^1/2$ hours. Drain. Beans can be cooked a day ahead, if desired, then covered and refrigerated.

3. Heat oven to 300 degrees. Cook bacon in a large flameproof casserole until crisp. Add onions and cook over medium heat, stirring often, until they are soft, 5 minutes. Remove from the heat and stir in the brown sugar, ketchup, maple syrup, Worcestershire sauce and mustard. Add beans and mix well.

4. Cover casserole and bake until beans are tender and well coated with a thick sauce, 2 to $2^1/2$ hours.

TUSCAN RICE AND BEANS

A versatile side dish that teams well with any grilled food, this rice and bean combo can be served hot or at room temperature.

Preparation time: 20 minutes
Soaking time: 12 hours or overnight
Cooking time: $1^1/2$ hours
Yield: 6 servings

---

1 cup dried white or navy beans

Water

3 tablespoons olive oil

1 medium onion, chopped

2 cloves garlic, minced

$^1/4$ cup chopped parsley

1 tablespoon chopped fresh basil, or $^1/2$ teaspoon dried

1 rib celery, minced

$^1/4$ cup minced smoked ham

$^1/4$ teaspoon red pepper flakes, optional

1 can (16 ounces) plum tomatoes, drained, coarsely chopped

Salt, freshly ground black pepper

1 cup rice, preferably short-grain Italian, cooked according to package directions

1. Cover the beans with a generous amount of cold water and soak 12 hours or overnight. Drain and place in a large pot; cover with water. Cook, partially covered, until just tender, 1 to $1^1/2$ hours.

2. Meanwhile, heat the oil in a skillet; add onion, garlic, parsley, basil, celery, ham and pepper flakes. Cook until vegetables are soft, 5 to 7 minutes. Add the tomatoes and season with salt and pepper. Cook gently for 10 minutes.

3. Add the vegetable mixture to the beans. Simmer gently about 15 minutes. Add cooked rice to bean mixture; mix well. Serve hot or at room temperature.

GRILLED GARDEN PASTA

There's something especially flavorful about vegetables cooked on the grill, and when they are nestled in pasta they take on new character. This easy recipe from Chicago Tribune *reader Patt Walt proves it.*

Preparation time: 25 minutes
Cooking time: 15 minutes
Yield: 4 servings

---

4 ripe tomatoes, halved crosswise

1 sweet onion, halved crosswise

1 large green bell pepper, quartered

2 tablespoons olive oil

1 pound pasta, such as rotini or penne, cooked according to package directions

2 cloves garlic, minced

1 cup fresh basil, chopped

1 cup grated Parmesan cheese

Salt, freshly ground pepper to taste

1. Brush tomatoes, onion and green pepper with olive oil. Grill over a hot fire until the vegetables are tender and beginning to brown at the edges, 8 to 10 minutes. Turn and grill 4 to 5 minutes longer. Remove from grill. When vegetables are cool enough to handle, chop coarsely.

2. Place hot pasta in a large bowl. Add garlic, basil, cheese, salt and pepper; mix well. Top with grilled vegetables. Serve hot or at room temperature.

KOREAN BEAN SPROUT SALAD

This salad boasts some vigorous Asian flavors but also would be at home at a Texas-style barbecue.

Preparation time: 15 minutes
Cooking time: 1 minute
Yield: 10 to 12 servings

1¹/₂ pounds fresh bean sprouts

Boiling water

3 green onions, chopped

2 tablespoons soy sauce

1 tablespoon Oriental sesame oil

2 teaspoons each: rice vinegar, roasted sesame seeds

Dash salt, chili oil or cayenne pepper

1 small red bell pepper, diced

1. Drop bean sprouts into a large pot of boiling water. Cook 1 minute. Immediately drain and rinse under cold water to stop the cooking. Drain well.

2. Place bean sprouts, green onions, soy sauce, sesame oil, vinegar, sesame seeds, salt and chili oil in large bowl. Toss well to mix. Sprinkle with red bell pepper. Refrigerate, stirring occasionally, up to 4 hours. Serve at room temperature.

Quickly seared on the grill, as pictured on the back cover, tropical fruit takes on an alluring sweet flavor. Try it with caramel sauce, or serve it plain with a bowl of ice cream or yogurt. Select fruits that are firm enough to hold their shape and cut them into large pieces.

Preparation time: 30 minutes
Cooking time: 3 to 7 minutes
Yield: 6 servings

---

1 fresh coconut

1 small ripe pineapple

1 papaya

1 large pink grapefruit

3 bananas

2 tablespoons unsalted butter, melted

1. Use an ice pick to poke out the eyes of the coconut; let the water inside drain out. Bake the coconut in a 400-degree oven for 20 minutes to crack the outer shell. Wrap the coconut securely in a towel and hit it with a hammer to remove the shell. Peel the thin brown skin off the meat with a vegetable peeler. Cut the meat into 8 to 10 pieces.

2. Core the pineapple and cut into spears. Cut the papaya in half lengthwise and scoop out the seeds. Slice into 6 to 8 wedges. Cut the grapefruit into 6 wedges. Peel the bananas and cut into chunks.

3. Brush all the fruit with melted butter. Grill over a medium fire, turning once, just until the fruit is heated. The pineapple, papaya, grapefruit and bananas will take only 3 to 4 minutes. The coconut will take 6 to 7 minutes.